CONCISE OFFICIAL HISTORY

of the

2nd Battalion
The Glasgow Highlanders
The Highland Light Infantry

The Naval & Military Press Ltd

Published by

The Naval & Military Press Ltd
Unit 10 Ridgewood Industrial Park,
Uckfield, East Sussex,
TN22 5QE England

Tel: +44 (0) 1825 749494
Fax: +44 (0) 1825 765701

www.naval-military-press.com
www.military-genealogy.com

Cover Image:
Infantrymen of the 2nd Battalion, Glasgow Highlanders, 15th (Scottish) Division,
with Churchill tanks of the 6th Guards Tank Brigade, near Moergestel, 26 October 1944.

This short account of the life of the 2nd Battalion The Glasgow Highlanders, The Highland Light Infantry, is dedicated to the memory of the freedom-loving men who, while serving with the Battalion, gave their lives for the preservation of democracy.

The main battles in which the Battalion fought:

CHEUX	BLERICK
ETERVILLE	GROOSEBECK
ESQUAY	MOYLAND WOOD
GHENT	BUCHOLT
BEST	HEGEMANNSKATH
LEENSEL WOOD	STADENSEN

UELZEN

CONTENTS

CHAPTER ONE

The 2nd Battalion The Glasgow Highlanders was born in April '39, one of the number of second-line Territorial Army Units brought into being in the aftermath of the Munich crises.

The first few days of the Unit were spent in Hotspur Street Drill Hall, Glasgow, where the ranks were mustered and the initial kit and equipment assembled prior to the war.

The first Commanding Officer was Lt-Col. T. G. Robinson, who had some years previously served with the 1st Battalion. Major (later Col.) G. Laird was 2 IC, Capt. (later Major) C. D. Gray Adjutant, and Lt. (later Capt.) I. M'L. MacLennen was Q.M.

From its inception the Battalion was noted for its spartan and comradely spirit, taking its place with the 10th and 11th Battalions HLI in the 46 (Highland) Infantry Brigade of the 15th (Scottish) Infantry Division.

The early training of the Battalion, which largely drew its men from the commercial houses of Glasgow, took place in Johnstone, Renfrewshire, and in Galashiels. Later the Battalion moved to Swindon and then to south-east Essex, being quartered during the summer and winter of 1940 in the villages of Rayleigh, Rochford, Billericay, Hockley and Canewdon.

In Essex the Battalion was operationally employed on Coast defences and airfield guards during the worst of the Blitz on this "bomb alley", and at the same time participated in many toughening exercises.

In February,1941, the Battalion moved to the beaches of Felixstowe, Suffolk, where almost every man had his special role in pillbox or dugout. However, under the leadership of Lt-Col. Robinson training went on. He believed in making the Unit one hundred per cent fit to attack, and was certainly not content that we should remain a defensive force. The Battalion took part in many large-scale exercises at this time.

In November, 1941, the Division moved to Northumberland, where the operational roles were lighter and the opportunities for Unit and formation training greater.

At this time Lt-Col. T. G. Robinson was appointed to the staff overseas and handed over command to Lt-Col. George Laird. Major Blackatter became 2IC for a few weeks before taking command of a Gordons Battalion, and his successor was Major Campbell Davies, M.C.

During its two years in Northumberland the Battalion moved from station to station, seeing successively Felton, Newcastle, Low Lynn, Berwick and Alnwick. This was probably the most difficult time the Unit had to face, as there were constant calls on it for drafts of officers and men for overseas. In these difficult conditions a high standard of training was maintained, a task rendered easier by the fine material in time drafted in to bring the Battalion up to strength.

In September, 1943, the 2nd Battalion moved to Bingley in Yorkshire, where it was brought up to strength and took part in final large-scale exercises such as "Blackcock" and "Eagle" in preparation for the task ahead.

By this time we knew we were training as a follow-up unit, that is to say our job would be to break out of a beachhead once the Second Front landings were secure.   .

At Berwick Lt-Col. P. U. Campbell took over command, and under his forceful and dynamic personality the final preparations went rapidly ahead, so that when we moved to Brighton, our D-Day concentration area, officers and men "had their tails right up". Highlight of our short stay there was our victory in the Brigade Sports, which we won for the third time.

On the Sixth day of June, 1944, the British Army went into battle. As the Battalion prepared to move off to the port of embarkation hundreds of bombers roared out to the coast of France, closely guarded convoys swept out from the shores across the Channel.

The day for which the Battalion had strived and trained had come; the morale of the men was at its highest as we started out on that long road which was to prove the last for so many brave and loyal comrades.

Following is the Order of Battle of the Battalion as it embarked for Normandy

Lt-Col. P. U. Campbell — Commanding Officer
Major J. C. Davies, MC — Second-in-Command
Capt. L. Ker Robertson — Adjutant
Lieut A. C. Bayvel — Intelligence Offr.
Capt. the Rev. J. S. Taylor, RAChD — Padre
Capt. S. Maw, RAMC — Medical Officer
RSM Endicott

HQ Company:

Capt. R. A. Taylor, OC — Capt. J. S. Stevens, QM
Lieut S. Dickson, SO — Lieut F. A. R. Wallace, MTO
RQMS Inglis — CSM Smythe
CQMS D. Sanders — PM M'Leod

Support Company:

Capt. E. M.C. Elliott, OC — Capt. W. Armstrong, Mortars
Capt. I. P. S. Wood, A/Tk — Capt. J. B. Johnstone, Carriers
Lieut T. Scott, A/Tk — Lieut A. M. Loudon, Carriers
Lieut J. Dunn, Pioneers — CSM Sheddon
CQMS Morton .

"A" Company:

Major B. Carson, OC
Capt. P. Floyd, 2IC (Residue)
Lieut R. T. Keeble
Lieut J. Kehoe
Lieut A. Smith (Can. Army)
CSM Tait
CQMS W. Sanders

"C" Company:

Major W. A. C. Lambie, OC
Capt. W. J. M. Renwick, 2IC
Lieut I. Waldie
Lieut W. Blackadder
Lieut J. Wark
CSM Moffatt
CQMS Driver

8

"B" Company:	"D" Company:
Major W. M. White, OC	Major C. D. Gray, OC
Capt. A. Miller, 2IC (Can. Army)	Capt. J. M. Anderson, 2IC
Lieut H. E. Rawlinson	Lieut K. Hollway
Lieut A. Renwick	Lieut A. Rennie
Lieut D. D. Hannah	Lieut J. Galloway
CSM Lane	CSM Johnstone
CQMS Simpson	CQMS M'Kendrick

It is regretted that owing to incomplete records it is not possible to give the names of all ranks who embarked. Officers are shown by the ranks they held at that time, and no mention is made here of the honours and awards won in later days.

9

THE RUINED FARMYARD USED AS BN RAP AT CHEUX

CHAPTER TWO

Into Battle

The rifle companies arrived off the coast of Normandy on the 17th June, concentrating in the area south of Vienne-en-Bessin. The remainder of the Battalion, with the transport and stores, had to remain seaborne off the beaches for a few days because of the storm which almost wrecked the improvised harbours. But the concentration of the Unit was completed in the evening of 24th June, when it was learned that the Division was going into the attack almost immediately to fulfill the role for which it had trained ——— a breakout from the bridgehead.

The Battalion moved to a Forward Assembly Area during the darkness of 24th/25th June, and final preparations for what we were then told was to be a big show were completed.

The objective of the Battalion was to be Cheux ——— "Chooks" it has always remained ——— a little village some three thousand yards south of the Canadian positions at Le Mesnil Patry. It was held by the 12th Panzer Div, and the route to the village lay through standing corn, compact little orchards, and by sunken tracks and hollows of dead ground. Little observation of the ground was possible, and full use had to be made of air photographs owing to the inadequacy of the maps.

The plan was for a three Battalion attack, the Glasgow Highlanders to take the village with the Cameronians on the right and the Royal Scots on the left. The artillery programme was to use six hundred

11

guns, and in addition there were several squadrons of medium and fighter bombers, the guns of the Royal Navy, and on the ground with us the Churchill tanks, the AVREs and the Flails.

At 0730 hours on the 26th of June the barrage opened, and ten minutes later the Battalion went into battle.

"C" and "D" Companies were forward, followed by "A" and "B", all closely supported by the tanks and moving right up with the barrage. The first opposition came in an area of two orchards bounded by thick hedges and fields of high corn, where the Germans had sewn anti-tank and -personnel mines liberally. Some of the tanks were knocked out, and on the right two of our carriers were blown up. Despite the mines the troops pushed through the orchards.

Beyond the. orchards "C" Company ran into heavy MG fire and were temporarily halted until they could clear the area. Meanwhile "D" Company pushed on through heavy enemy mortar fire to assault and clear a small wood screening Cheux.

During the further course of the advance the Companies continued to destroy the enemy lurking in the ditches and hedges, a process which naturally lost the Battalion the advantage of the barrage and a closely integrated front.

About 0930 hours "D" Company reported the capture of the village, and by 1000 hours all Companies were in positions given on the spot by Col. Campbell. The enemy's counter-attack by fire was vigorous and unceasing for the remainder of the morning, but the troops re-organised and dug-in like veterans.

The RAP opened in a barn beside Bn HQ on the outskirts of the smouldering ruin which had been Cheux, and here the Medical Officer and Padre dealt with the casualties of half-a-dozen units. While casualties were coming in and ambulances nosed in and out German mortars poured bombs into the blazing farmhouse, a grim and ugly scene.

For twenty-four hours the Battalion held the village while supporting armour and infantry moved into position on the flanks for a further bite into the German positions. During this time the forward troops were continually harassed by snipers, who, because of the closeness of the country, could approach to within twenty yards of our positions; and for the whole Battalion there was little respite from mortaring and air-burster shelling.

The advance to Cheux demanded the utmost disregard for their persons from the men; during the fighting outstanding bravery was shown by Lt. J. Wark, "C" Company, who went in alone to destroy enemy MG posts, by Cpl. Shaw, "D" Company, who, although wounded, killed four Germans in a post and captured four others, and by CSM (later Lieut) Tait, who showed great coolness in reorganising "A" Company under fire.

Three officers and 19 other ranks were killed and six officers and 178 other ranks wounded and missing, of whom a high percentage later succumbed to their wounds.

After Cheux

The Battalion was withdrawn into dead ground behind Cheux to reorganise, and was ordered forward to occupy the orchard-village of Colleville the same afternoon.

In defensive positions at Colleville the Battalion had its first experience of "Moaning Minnies", the "nebelwerfer" multibarrelled mortars the Germans concentrated around the tip of the "Scottish Corridor", as the salient became called.

REFUGEES
PASSING OUR
CARRIERS
ON THE WAY
TO COLLEVILLE

13

The following day, June 28th, the Battalion was ordered to move two miles west to the charred ruins of the village of Mondrainville, where a two-day tank battle had been fought with the utmost viciousness. Just before the Battalion moved, the infantry, supported by tanks, drove off a German attack supported by Tiger tanks. Our own mortars here knocked out two enemy mortar positions, and identification of wounded showed that we were facing the 2nd Bn Der Fuhrer Regt of the 2nd SS Panzer Div. During the fighting Lt Loudon was killed leading a carrier group in dismounted action.

The Battalion dug in at Mondrainville and faced heavy enemy mortaring on a slight forward slope outside the village. On the 29th our Padre, the Rev James S. Taylor, was killed when the RAP truck received a direct hit. He had been the Battalion Padre for almost five years and was greatly loved by all ranks.

At Mondrainville the Battalion had its first experience of Tiger tanks at close quarters, but the CO called up Churchills and although the tank battle was fought literally over the heads of the infantry the Germans were driven off.

The Battalion was relieved on the night of 30th June under cover of a heavy artillery barrage, which was later discovered to have knocked out large numbers of Germans seemingly preparing for an attack on our positions.

The Battalion came out to rest half as strong in numbers as when it set off to take Cheux. It had gained enormously in prestige and confidence, and was justifiably proud of the knock it had given the Storm Troopers, the cream of Rommel's forces in Normandy.

Eterville and Esquay

On the 10th of July the Battalion again went into the attack. On that morning the Canadians were scheduled to take Caen, and the Brigade task was to clear and protect the right flank of the town.

The Battalion advanced in the early morning along the main Bayeux-Caen road, through Verson, to the outskirts of the hamlet of Bretteville-Sur-Odon, clearing the north bank of the river Odon with the Seaforths: there was little opposition.

14

In the afternoon of the 10th the Canadians took over our positions and we were placed on a reverse slope behind the Cameronians, who were put into the hamlet of Eterville, south-west of smouldering Caen. In these positions our carriers suffered casualties from mortaring, which was extremely heavy as the enemy fought desperately to throw the Cameronians out of Eterville.

Late that night Major Campbell Davies took over command of the Cameronians for a short time, as their CO had been slightly wounded, and early the following morning our "C" Company, commanded by Major W. A. C. Lambie, was ordered to move forward to hold the left flank of Eterville. They suffered heavy casualties taking and holding this position, which was very open and under direct enemy observation for a time.

At about 1400 hours the Battalion was ordered to relieve the Cameronians. The rifle companies were in exposed positions around the tiny village and subject to continuous sniping. The enemy made full use of the standing corn all around the village and time and again attempted infiltration into our lines.

That night The Battalion was withdrawn into a Divisional concentration area, Canadians taking over the village. At Eterville we suffered 85 killed and wounded.

Following reorganisation the Battalion was detailed for a special role under command of 227 Bde. This was to be a "last light attack" on the village of Esquay, some 2000 yards south of the Odon. This attack was to hold a pivotal point for the Divisional attack down to the river Orne.

The Bde attack failed, and for two days the Battalion remained far out in front of other British units, holding desperately to positions barely screened from full enemy view.

In the evening of 15th July the Bn moved to the attack, supported by one battalion Churchills, one troop AVREs, one troop Crocodiles (Churchill flamethrowers), and one company MMGs. Owing to enemy shelling and mortaring the advance across the open ground in front of Esquay was slower than anticipated, and it was full darkness before the troops swept through the village.

15

LEADING INFANTRY PASSING THROUGH VERSON ON THE WAY TO ETERVILLE

In this operation searchlights shining on to the clouds provided the first "artificial moonlight" of the war. They were needed; the plan was for the Companies to destroy the enemy in and around the village and then to take up defensive positions a few hundred yards away, on higher ground north-east of Esquay.

The enemy was routed. He didn't like the bayonets in the gloom and he didn't like the searing flames of the Crocodiles. When dawn came the Battalion was dug in, anti-tank guns were in position, and our supporting tanks had concentrated in dead ground a thousand yards to the rear. During the night the Battalion Pioneers had laid a minefield to cover our left forward flank.

By daylight we found that some positions were within hand-grenade distance of German slits, and that almost every platoon area was overlooked. So for most of that day the artillery were kept busy keeping the enemy off his OP line and smoking his forward areas.

It was an impossibility to move in the Battalion area during the Sunday of 16th July. It was a day of glaring heat, and the Battalion was toasted in its shallow slits; no water came up, a fact which annoyed the Battalion more than the moaning minnies. "A" Company on the right flank was in contact with strong enemy armoured patrols most of this day but held its ground although depleted in numbers. The stretcher bearers worked wonders getting the wounded away, having to make very long carries.

To the south of Esquay the Battalion could see into the heart of the German defences, and well-directed artillery fire caused havoc to his concentrating forces. Our own mortars fired 1500 rounds this day, although reduced to three.

During one of many "A" Company "parties" Sgt Blair knocked out two enemy Mk 1V tanks at a range of a few yards, and Sgts Duncan and Gillespie distinguished themselves by leading patrols into enemy positions.

A reorganisation of Company positions followed a very strong but not very clever counter-attack by the Germans at last light. Our supporting tanks and our own infantry arms caused very heavy casualties at extremely short range. New positions were dug in darkness and in the first few hours of daylight on 17th July, when there was a thick morning mist.

In daylight the Commanding Officer continued his work of the previous day in directing arty fire on observed enemy movement. For a time the troops had a grandstand view of the German scuttling for safety some thousands of yards south of Esquay. No actual enemy attack was mounted against the Battalion this second day, as our arty and mortar fire was heavy and accurate.

That night the Battalion was relieved and returned, very tired but proud, to Mondrainville. Casualties in the attack itself were amazingly light ——— three killed and 21 wounded.

At Mondrainville the Battalion met with only long-range shelling and mortaring, in which there was lost Major Murray White, an original Glasgow Highlander and gallant soldier.

The Break Through

Without participating in any further large-scale attack the Battalion spent the rest of July in and out of the line in the area of Caumont, latterly preparing for the Divisional battle of the 30th July. This attack developed into a series of short advances through villages south of Caumont, it being gradually appreciated that the enemy was withdrawing in some strength. During these advances on small features and villages the Battalion had the support of tanks in some numbers but often had to operate without them owing to the difficult nature of the ground.

On 19th August the Battalion was south-west of Falaise in a reasonably quiet area, and an opportunity was taken to reorganise the Pipe Band under Sgt Chisholm, Pipe Major M'Leod having been wounded at Verson.

On 24th August the Battalion really got started on the moves which were to take it across the Seine, the Albert Canal, and the Rhine into the heart of Germany.

24th August: to east of Bierre — 25th August: to L'Oraille

26th August: to Emanville — 27th August: to Vieux Villers, near the Seine

The dark and stormy days of Normandy were over. The British Army was on the move, on foot and wheels, in tanks and carriers and TCVs. And in the forefront of this spear of steel and high endeavour were The Glasgow Highlanders.

HONOURS and AWARDS

BAR to DSO
Lt/Col. H. C. Baker-Baker, DSO, MBE

DSO
Lt/Col. P. U. Campbell

MC
Major C. D. Gray
,,   H. R. Stobbs
,,   W. Armstrong
,,   G. P. Earnshaw
Lieut. J. A. Wark
,,   D. J. Tait
,,   C. R. McLellan

MM
Csm   J. Bell
Sgt   A. Shaw
,,   D. Temple
,,   P. Pimblett
,,   S. Tait
L/Sgt   Tordoff
Cpl   J. Hamilton
,,   G. Bennett
,,   Tye
Pte   J. Atrinson
,,   H. Sadler
,,   J. Bell
,,   J. Williams

U.S. BRONZE MEDAL
Sgt   G. Robb

FRENCH
CROIX de GUERRE
Major A. F. Smith
Sgt   J. Blair

ORDER of LEOPOLD and
CROIX de GUERRE
Major R. A. Taylor

MENTIONS
in DESPATCHES
Major G. P. Earnshaw
,,   W. Armstrong
,,   W. J. M. Renwick
Lieut. J. A. Galloway
,,   D. H. M. Forbes
,,   T. R. H. McLaren
CSM.   J. Bell
Sgt.   G. Robb
,,   F. Kilday
,,   J. Gillespie
CPL.   G. Mackay

ROLL OF ✝ HONOUR

Officers

Major	W M White	"B"	Coy
	J M Anderson	"D"	Coy
	A C Hamilton	"C"	Coy
,,	J C Stanton	"C"	Coy
Capt	I P S Wood	"S"	Coy
Capt/Rev	J S Taylor	Padre	
Capt	T Scott	"S"	Coy
Lieut	W Blackadder	"C"	Coy
	A M Loudon	"S"	Coy
	R T Keeble	"A"	Coy
	W J Waldie	"C"	Coy
	F A R Wallace	"HQ"	Coy
	D D Hannah	"HQ"	Coy
	J Dunn	"S"	Coy
	A J Renwick	"C"	Coy
	C B Kendall	"A"	Coy
	J B Matthew	"B"	Coy.

Other Ranks

Sjt	Marsh	R	Cpl	Thorley	D	Pte	Richards	G
	Wood	R	Lcpl	Charlesworth			Barrie	D
	Muskett	G	,,	Garnett	G		Smith	R
,,	Whittingham		Pte	Middleton	G	,,	Spencer	C
Cpl	Maitland	E		Edwards	A		Wallace	F
	Sanders	D		Milligan	G		Scott	C
	Grosse	R		Low	A		Glover	E
	Buchanan	R		Edmondson	A		McCarthy	J
	Arthur	W						

20

Rank	Name	Init.	Rank	Name	Init.	Rank	Name	Init.
Pte	Kean	F	Pte	Powell	R	Sgt	White	L
,,	Martin	W	,,	Thompson	H	CSM	Moffat	W
,,	Lane	F	,,	Read	R	Cpl	Ritchie	C
,,	Duffield		,,	Adams	J	,,	Pretlove	A
Sjt.	Bowman	W	,.	Winn	J	L/Sgt	Stirton	L
L/C	Brown	F	,,	Ainscow	E	Cpl	Atkinson	W
Pte	Kidd	A	,,	Miller	S	,,	Davies	J
,,	Hamilton	W	,,	Barber	C	,,	Ure	A
,,	Mungall	W	,,	Worrall	J	,,	Auton	L
,,	Carmichael	J	,,	Salmon	L	L/C	Taylor	B
,,	Kilner	L	,,	Pendle	D	,,	White	V
,,	Livingstone	T	,,	Scheffler	H	,,	Dodd	F
,,	Anderson	R	Sgt	Jackson	C	,,	Quinn	J
,,	Robb	A	,,	Scott	W	,,	Turner	J
,,	Leishman	G	Cpl	Aspell	R	,,	Robinson	R
,,	Robinson	R	,,	Cooper	G	,,	Bridgeman	G
Pte	Lloyd	G	,,	McKinley	I	Pte	Kaye	E
,,	Adams	R	,,	Harris	G	,,	Riddell	T
,,	Jones	W	L/C	Humber	A	,,	Schofield	D
,,	McGouldrick	J	,,	Young	H	,,	Inglis	J
,,	Evans	W	,,	Sumner	D	,,	Savins	G
,,	Latimer	W	Pte	Gee	L	,,	Hill	L
,,	Lovegrove	R	,,	Horn	E	,,	Nunnerley	H
,,	Cullen	J	,,	Hulse	W	,,	Radcliffe	S
C.S.M.	Payne	F	,,	Macfarlane	A	,,	Gaunt	C
Sgt.	Strang	A	,,	Angel	R	,,	Wright	K
,,	Murphy	E		Parry	R	,,	McLoughlin	R
Cpl.	Ferguson	A		Pearson	F	,,	Wright	L
L/Sgt.	Duncan	A		Erskine	J	,,	Bean	C
Cpl	Firth	W		McKinley	T	,,	Tranter	J
L/Cpl	Morton	J	,,	Gormley	J	,,	Large	G
L/Cpl	Lamb	C	,,	Huddison	A	,,	Bready	C
,,	Wrennall	F	,,	Crangle	W	,,	Cumming	R
,,	Orr	H	,,	Tobin	W	,,	Wright	H
Pte	Verbitsky	J	Sgt	Walker	D	,,	Irving	M
,,	Davies	H	CSM	Walsh	A	,,	Gaish	C

Pte	Yagernose	A	Pte	Gunn	H	Pte	Richardson	H
,,	Ashworth	F	,,	Park	A	,,	Rodger	J
,,	Davies	C	,,	Scott	A	,,	Kirk	T
,,	Irwin	B	,,	Evans	A	,,	Smith	J
,,	Marshall	E	,,	Raper	F	,,	Lane	F
,,	Hushion	J	,,	Keenan	H	,,	Smith	T
,,	Bidwell	B	,,	Thorpe	T	,,	Trevey	J
,,	Ault	J	,,	Smith	H	,,	Grady	L
,,	Broadley	W	,,	Wilson	E	,,	Cornell	F
C/Sgt	McKendrick	J	,,	Roe	A	,,	Anderson	A
Sgt	Beattie	W	,,	Raybould	F	,,	Phillips	F
Sgt	Kinealy	E	,,	Hardman	R	,,	Kirkland	G
,,	Turner	A	,,	Chapman	F	,,	Herrick	T
L/Sgt	Hastings	A	,,	Green	H	,,	Lloyd	G
,,	Butterworth	W	,,	Mersh	J	,,	Lund	T
Cpl	Chinskie	P	,,	Tipping	G	,,	Sutherland	G
,,	Halley	J	,,	Cooper	F	,,	Boyd	W
,,	Whyte	A	,,	Dresser	H	,,	Stevenson	L
,,	Anderson	G	,,	Keddy	A	,,	Dix	C
,,	Cope	J	,,	Neary	W	,,	Toplis	L
,,	Jones	F	,,	Woodhouse	H	,,	Jennings	U
L/C	Shelley	W	,,	Cobain	A	,,	Lundie	R
,,	Smith	A		McGraw	J	,,	Byrne	J
,,	Hubbard	G		Cutmore	E	L/Cpl	Davies	W
,,	Thomson	D		Williams	I.			
,,	Bandy	F		McLean	J			

CHAPTER THREE

The Battle for Ghent

Up to the first week in September, '44, the Battalion was committed to no major action but moved on with the bulk of the British infantry and armour to make contact with the retreating enemy.

In the little town of Belleghem, on 5th September, the Commanding Officer was presented with a magnificent tapestry portrait of H. M. King George VI; this had been kept hidden during the war for presentation to the liberating unit.

On 9th September the Battalion concentrated south of Ghent, under command of 131 Inf Bde, to prepare for the onslaught on the canal sector held in strength. The enemy was firmly established in factories and houses, where the civilians were a hindrance to an all-out battle, and although he had no tanks he had bazookas, spandaus and 88 mm guns well forward in the streets, with mortars and big guns, including railway guns, further back.

This was the Battalion's first experience of street and factory fighting on a large scale. On the way up to the FUP "B" Company suffered casualties when a TCV received a direct shell hit.

The rifle companies moved into the attack in the early evening. Each had been given a sector across the canal to clear, the final objective being the line of the railway. To begin with progress was slow as each barred and shuttered house had to be searched from cellar to attic. "C" Company spent some time clearing the asylum, which was a warren of rooms and passages. On "D" Company's front a factory housing many Germans was left until the following morning.

By nightfall the Battalion had taken 14 prisoners and killed many more of the enemy.

On 10th September the street fighting recommenced at dawn and proceeded with great intensity all day. The Battalion support included Shermans, M10s and MMGs, and our own supporting weapons, chiefly the Carrier Platoon, were fully employed helping companies forward. 17 Platoon of "D" Company made a memorable assault on the factory and captured two officers and 198 other ranks.

Number 18 Platoon, "D" Company, commanded by Sgt (later Lieut) M'Laren, had paused to reorganise at one stage when they were vigorously attacked by about 80 Germans from three directions. Number 7045793 Pte Albert Evans was ordered to cover two roads with his Bren while the Platoon withdrew. Evans was wounded by Spandau fire almost immediately but refused to be evacuated. He kept his gun in action and died at his post, having covered his comrades back, killed 10 Germans and wounded many more.

A Belgian eye-witness wrote of this incident: "Never in my life will I forget the bravery of that fine British soldier, whom I saw fighting and dying as a hero."

"C" Company were held up at the approches to a large cemetery, which was defended in strength, and which was also an obstacle to the advance of "B" Company. This day the Battalion captured a total of six officers and 233 other ranks.

On the 11th further house-clearing continued although the main body of the enemy withdrew, and in the evening the Glasgow Highlanders were relieved. The battle had been fought mainly on the platoon level, at close quarters and hampered by half-crazed civilians. We lost 10 killed and 56 wounded.

On 13th September the Battalion crossed the Albert Canal south of Gheel, on the 21st to Eindhoven, in Holland, and then up to the Wilhelmina Canal for the attack on Best.

The Battle of Best

The Battalion went into the assault on the the southern reaches of Best at noon on 22nd September. In the initial phase "A" Company came under withering fire and two platoons were tied to the ground. On all company fronts casualties were suffered from aimed MG fire, and at darkness the forward infantry were still fighting for their objectives. "D" Company drove the enemy from a monastery at dusk.

The Battalion attack continued with murderous intensity the following day. Both "C" and "D" Companies reached their objectives, the line of the railway, in the evening, and spent the night with the railway embankment separating them from the defenders.

At about 0700 hours on the morning of the 24th the CSM of "B" Company arrived wounded at Bn HQ to report that his Company had been overwhelmed by a strong attack. Simultaneously all companies, including a company of the Cameronians under command, reported heavy enemy counter-attacks. These were held although the line had to be shortened to prevent infiltration.

It appears that "B" Company were subjected to heavy bazooka fire at point-blank range and were then rushed. Only six men were accounted for, and when the Battalion was relieved the strengths were: "A" 54, two officers, "B" 6, "C" 51, one officer, "D" 43, no officers.

Major Miller, OC "B" Company, was known to be wounded, and was found in an air-raid shelter the following day by the Cameronians.

Losses in this battle were 138, which included 50 missing; up to the end of the month the Germans continued to hold the ground north of the railway line, which objective had been secured earlier by the Battalion.

CHAPTER FOUR

Rest and Training

At the beginning of October the Battalion was withdrawn to Helmond for rest and training, the latter following the arrival of reinforcements.

On the 20th of the month the Commanding Officer, Lt-Col. P. U. Campbell, DSO, vacated command of the Unit. He had led the Battalion with distinction and gallantry, and had been for some months the only remaining commanding officer in the Division who had landed with his men in Normandy. He was succeeded until the end of the month by Major J. C. Davies, M.C., who in turn handed over command to Lt-Col. H. C. Baker-Baker, DSO, MBE.

On 24th October the Battalion, reformed and rested, moved out of Helmond with tanks. Little serious opposition was encountered until reaching the village of Oisterwijke, where a two-battalion attack drove in the defences. Here "C" Company were held up and with the cross fire of "D" Company put in a classic attack on a large block of factory buildings.

On the same afternoon the Carrier Platoon used wasp flamethrowers most effectively against a strongpoint on "B" Company's flank. This was the first time the weapon had been used in the Division.

On the following day the Battalion entered Tilburg, to receive a most enthusiastic welcome from the Dutch.

Counter-Attack: Leensel

On 29th October the Battalion was hurriedly moved to Leensel Wood to take part in repelling the heavy German counter-attack

which had already attained some measure of success. The exhausted Americans holding this sector had suffered heavy casualties in men and tanks, and were withdrawn.

In darkness the rifle companies in patrol formation were put into the wood, which was being shelled and mortared in places by the enemy. By 2200 hours the Battalion had taken up firm positions without encountering the Germans. During the night our patrols found enemy to the east of our positions.

In the early morning an enemy force was surprised forming up near the Battalion lines, and devastating artillery fire was brought to bear on it. At about 1000 hours the forward companies were shelled and mortared on a scale reminiscent of Eterville and Esquay, and on the fire lifting "B" and "D" Companies were attacked by infantry supported by SP guns.

Initially the enemy had no success, but when he commenced infiltrating in strength into the undefended woods south of our lines the situation became increasingly serious. It was then apparent that the enemy was in some numbers behind the Battalion, while stronger attacks were being mounted in front.

The arrival of reinforcing companies from the Royal Scots and the Royal Scots Fusiliers, together with two troops of tanks, enabled

27

the Battalion to stabilise its line. About 50 casualties were incurred in this action at a much greater cost to the enemy. Following this battle in the woods the Battalion was taken forward banks of the Wilhelmina Canal to protect the west flank of the Division.

Deception at Blerick

Most of November was spent on the Canal line in patrolling operations; on 21st November we crossed the Deurne Canal, and on the 29th were moved south to the woods north-west of Blerick, on the west bank of the River Maas facing Venlo.

Here the Battalion had the role of deceiving the enemy by constant strong patrolling away from the direction of the Divisional attack on Blerick. One particularly effective patrol from "B" Company penetrated the enemy defences and inflicted casualties.

So successful was the Battalion in this task that when the attack on Blerick took place on 3rd December the Glasgow Highlanders absorbed most of the German arty and mortar defensive fire.

The Advance from Nijmegen

From 3rd December, '44, to 8th February, '45, the Battalion was almost fully employed on "the watch on the Maas." On the latter date it went into the forefront of the battle for the gapping of the Siegfried Line.

In this battle there was used the heaviest arty programme ever employed in an Allied operation. It is not surprising, therefore, that the enemy gave little opposition, most of our casualties being incurred in minefields. During the day 230 prisoners were taken.

On the 9th and 10th the Battalion held its position before moving to Cleve on the 11th. Cleve was vacated on 14th February to mount an attack on the defended woods south-east of Rosendahl. The village was occupied without much opposition, but on moving through to take the high ground which was the final objective "C" Company suffered many casualties.

With "A" Company on their objective "B" Company were pushed through to take the ground on the right and succeeded in getting one

ON THE ALERT AT BLERICK

29

platoon forward. This platoon faced a bitter counter-attack and destroyed a SP gun with a piat at 50 yards range. The ground was held that night, and the following day flanking attacks by the Seaforths and Cameronians enabled the Battalion to make its full advance.

On 16th February the Battalion was ordered to attack Moyland Schloss, a mediaeval castle with deep moats. During the planning stage for this operation the Commanding Officer had the assistance of an Allied officer whose home the castle had been.

The attack on the castle was cancelled and the Battalion returned to Cleve, there to prepare for the attack on Bucholt. For this operation "B" and "D" Companies used Kangaroos, the heavy armour of which prevented many casualties from shelling and mortaring.

This was a short and sharp engagement in which the Battalion suffered 30 casualties, mostly from enemy shelling, which was as fierce as it was accurate. 150 prisoners were taken.

The attack on Bucholt was followed by wood-clearing south of Schloss Kalbeck on 22nd February, and on 25th February the Battalion was withdrawn for rest.

CHAPTER FIVE

The Rhine Crossing and Beyond

The Glasgow Highlanders were in reserve for the assault crossing of the Rhine, and it was not until they were well inside the bridgehead, at Haffen, on 24th March, that opposition was met. Both here and in the wooded country in the area of the Mehr lakes the Battalion had to fight hard for its ground.

On 27th March the Battalion faced German 88 mm and flak guns at point-blank range during their attack on the farm of Hegemannskath, and at nightfall only two companies had gained their objectives. The following day the enemy pulled out, and the further advance of the Battalion was through country littered with abandoned German equipment and decorated with white flags.

At this time the great retreat of the German forces was gaining momentum, and on 12th April the Battalion was formed into a striking force to give it greater mobility. This "group" consisted of the Glasgow Highlanders, a squadron of tanks from 4th Bn The Coldstream Guards, 190 Field Regiment, MMGs, heavy mortars and other supporting arms. The only initial opposition to our movement occurred at Marnede, where "A" Company cleared a wood of stubborn defenders.

In the evening of the 14th the Battalion harboured in the small town of Stadensen, where perimeter defences were set up. No enemy were suspected in the area, but at 0400 hours on the 15th "B" Company reported the noise of tracked vehicles approaching. Within a matter of minutes the Germans had their SPs in the village, and in the grim

B N HQ TRANSPORT AFTER THE BATTLE OF STADENSEN

darkness all the terrors and confusion of street-fighting ensued. All the houses in our hands were defended and fought for with the utmost bitterness as the enemy systematically poured fire into them. Within a very short time the village was ablaze, a factor which mitigated against German success. Up to this time the defenders were at a disadvantage owing to the darkness.

One German battle group hit Bn HQ, another our soft transport, which burned fiercely. All over the town the Jocks came to grips with the German, each little battle lit up as in a fantastic stage play. In the middle of this inferno the RAP———the MO, Padre and stretcher-bearers ——— carried on ministering to the wounded although the houses were aflame around them.

The perimeter forces were reinforced by tanks, and by 0630 hours, the enemy having failed to dislodge the Battalion or increase his forces, the situation began to be mastered. At daylight our anti-tank guns went into action and accounted for 10 enemy SP guns, and by 0900 hours all the enemy in the perimeter had been accounted for and all fresh attacks repulsed.

From prisoners and captured documents it was learned that this enemy force was the advance guard of the newly-formed and equipped Panzer Div Clausewitz, the last German offensive effort. In this engagement they left behind 12 SP guns, 10 armoured half-tracks, many killed and a large number of prisoners. Our casualties were five killed, including Capt. Tom Scott and Lieut Andrew Renwick, and 47 wounded and missing.

The Last Days

18th April found the Battalion in its last major engagement, the clearing of the town of Uelzen. There was little opposition, as the men dealt with the snipers in houses with the utmost ruthlessness. After Stadensen the Jocks were in no mood for half-measures.

As for the Rhine crossing the Battalion was in reserve for the assault on the river Elbe, and again it was in breaking out of the bridgehead that enemy were met. It was, however, insufficient to cause serious delay or casualties.

33

STREET FIGHTING IN UELZEN

On 2nd May the Battalion took part in the clearing of the vast Sachsenwald forest, where large numbers of greatly dispirited prisoners were taken.

On the night of 5th May, '45, the Battalion was told of the total surrender of the German forces. The job was done, and from then until the 31st March, '46, the Battalion was a Garrison force.

It had been a long and bitter road from the beaches of Normandy to the vital heart of Germany, but a road from which the Battalion never turned aside nor on which it ever faltered.

Its battles and work in patrolling and defence have been all too briefly mentioned in this book, which has concentrated in ennumerating the main engagements which brought it honour and distinction.

The casualty lists were the longest of any Battalion in the 15th (Scottish) Division: officers ——— 17 killed, 34 wounded, one missing; other ranks ——— 207 killed, 798 wounded, 47 missing.

It is the wish of all ranks that the 2nd Bn The Glasgow Highlanders on disbandment will be remembered chiefly for the sacrifices of their comrades.

www.ingramcontent.com/pod-product-compliance
Lightning Source LLC
LaVergne TN
LVHW010306070426
835509LV00030B/3500